STIRLING CASTLE

Fun FACTS & Amazing ACTIVITIES

Illustrated by Moreno Chiacchiera

Kelpies World

HISTORIC ENVIRONMENT SCOTLAND

ÀRAINNEACHD EACHDRAIDHEIL ALBA

Castle Guide

Welcome to Stirling Castle. Enjoy exploring its history and discovering fun facts!

FUN FACTS

The castle wasn't always made of stone. It was mainly wooden until the 1380s.

The Ladies' Lookout got its name because noblewomen stood there to watch knights jousting.

A Gaelic legend says a fairy built Stirling Castle...

... then turned into a fireball!

Gruesome Castle — p.26

Young Mary, Queen of Scots — p.18

The Stirling Heads — p.12

Building a Royal Palace — p.10

Games and Sports — p.20

Unicorns at Stirling — p.14

Under Siege! — p.6

p.4 — Scottish Heroes at Stirling

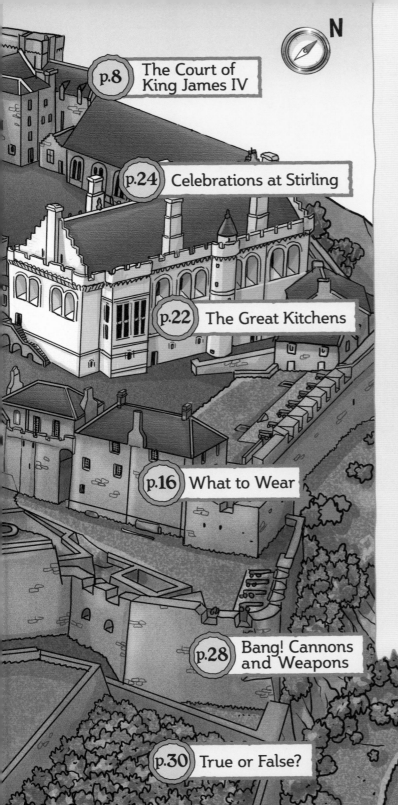

N

p.8 The Court of King James IV

p.24 Celebrations at Stirling

p.22 The Great Kitchens

p.16 What to Wear

p.28 Bang! Cannons and Weapons

p.30 True or False?

Stirling on the map

Stirling Castle was very important because it guarded the route between northern and southern Scotland. It can be seen on a map of Britain from 1250, which is the oldest map made of Scotland. Back then, mapmakers had to guess shapes and distances. They didn't get it quite right!

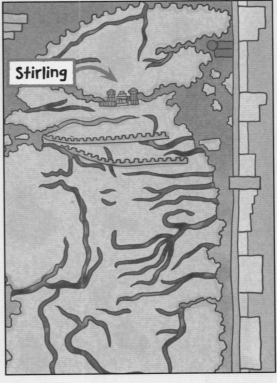

Stirling

Where's Isla?

Isla the unicorn is hiding on every page. Can you spot her?

Scottish Heroes at Stirling

William Wallace and Robert the Bruce are famous heroes of the Scottish Wars of Independence. Each won important battles near Stirling Castle.

1296: The English king Edward I wanted to rule Scotland too, so he invaded. Scotland and England were at war!

1297: Scottish warrior William Wallace cleverly defeated the English at the Battle of Stirling Bridge, close to Stirling Castle.

1305: Wallace was captured! King Edward I called him a traitor and had him executed.

I could not be a traitor to Edward, for he was never my king!

1306: Yet the fight for Scotland's freedom went on. A nobleman called Robert Bruce was crowned king of Scots.

1314: King Robert won the Battle of Bannockburn. Later, Scotland became an independent country again.

Today: Both heroes are honoured in Stirling. There is a statue of Robert the Bruce outside the castle, and you can see the National Wallace Monument from the walls.

Choose the right route

Help William Wallace's army choose the right route from the top of Abbey Craig to the battlefield at Stirling Bridge.

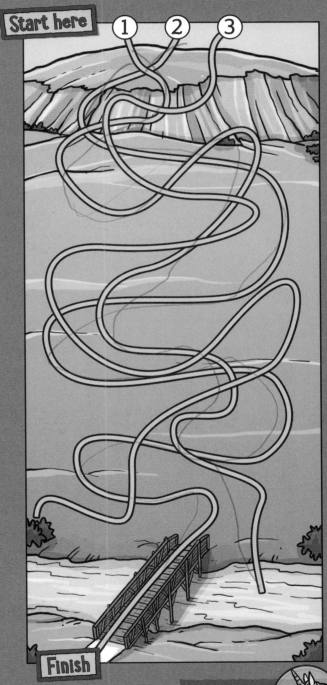

Start here

① ② ③

Finish

Where's Isla?

Under Siege!

Stirling Castle was captured 8 times in 50 years! In 1304, during the Scottish Wars of Independence, King Edward I of England laid siege to the castle using a terrifying giant trebuchet called War Wolf. Just 30 soldiers defended Stirling Castle for 3 whole months.

How to defend

Drop rocks, boiling oil and even poo on attackers.

How to attack

Smash the gate with a battering ram.

Shoot lots of arrows at the defenders.

Stop food arriving so the defenders grow hungry and weak.

Destroy the gatehouse with War Wolf!

Damage the walls with stones launched from mangonels (a kind of catapult).

How to fire a trebuchet

A trebuchet (tre-boo-shay) was like a giant slingshot that hurled rocks to break down castle walls. It was one of the deadliest weapons in medieval warfare.

① Load large rocks into the sling.

② Drop the heavy counterweight...

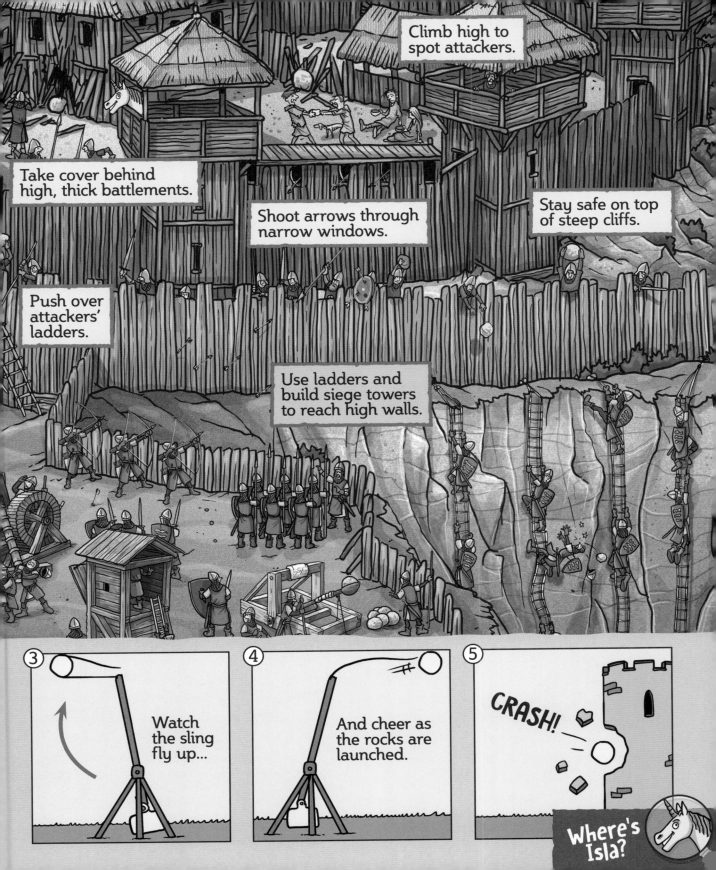

The Court of King James IV

James IV was king of Scotland from 1488 to 1513 and lived at Stirling Castle. He enjoyed art, music and science, and invited lots of different people to show off their talents at his court in the Great Hall.

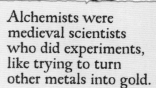

Peter the Moor was one of James IV's courtiers. Historical records show that Black people have lived in Scotland for hundreds of years. A 'Moor', or 'More', was an old-fashioned name for someone of African descent.

Alchemists were medieval scientists who did experiments, like trying to turn other metals into gold.

The 'Moorish Lassies', Ellen and Margaret, were probably taken from North Africa as young girls and later became ladies-in-waiting and important members of James IV's court.

Legend has it that John Damian, James IV's alchemist, built wings from chicken feathers and tried to fly to France!

It would have worked if I'd used eagle feathers!

But he landed in a dung heap and broke his leg!

Search the court
How many goblets can you find in the court?

Clever James IV learned 7 languages. He was the last king to speak Scottish Gaelic.

Only jesters were allowed to be cheeky to the king!

James IV built the Forework, a fairytale-like entrance to the castle, to show people he was a rich, important king.

Musicians played lutes, recorders and clarsachs (a type of harp).

Scottish poets were called 'makars'. They had poetry battles called 'flytings'.

Dancers entertained the court.

Where's Isla?

Building a Royal Palace

After James IV died, his son James V continued to improve Stirling Castle. In the 1540s King James V built the Royal Palace for his new queen, Marie de Guise. She was very impressed — and so was everyone else!

Lion

The lion shows that James V was strong and brave.

Musician

Musicians show that James V wanted people to enjoy music and dancing.

James V

Ganymede

Venus

Sculptures cover the palace walls. Each says something about the kind of king James V was.

The Greek gods and goddesses show that James V wanted Scotland to be wealthy and peaceful.

Saturn

Abundance

I5 stands for 'Iacobus V', which is Latin for James V.

The Royal Palace has been restored to how it first looked in the 1540s. The project took more than 10 years and cost over £12 million.

Spot the difference

This statue shows James V dressed like a wise old prophet – though in real life his beard never grew that long! Can you find 5 differences between these 2 statues?

James V had lots of exotic pets, including a lion. He might have kept it in part of the Royal Palace called the Lion's Den.

Where's Isla?

The Stirling Heads

Inside the Royal Palace, James V had the ceiling of the King's Inner Chamber decorated with the amazing Stirling Heads. Carved from wood, the 41 heads showed the kind of king he wanted to be. They included people from history and legendary characters – and even James V himself!

James V is wearing his wedding coat, sewn with 50,000 pearls, to show he was a rich and stylish king.

James V celebrated his marriage to **Marie de Guise** by showing her carrying wedding flowers.

The jester shows James V wanted people to know he enjoyed fun and laughter!

James V wanted people to think he was great and wise like the mythical hero **Hercules**.

the story of the Stirling Heads

1777: The 200-year-old ceiling collapsed and a soldier was badly injured. The governor of Stirling Prison saved the fallen Heads from being used as firewood, but lots of them were broken, given away or lost.

1817: When royalty no longer lived in Stirling Castle, the British army took over. Jane Ferrier was married to the castle's Deputy Governor. She tracked down and illustrated many of the lost Stirling Heads.

Doodle

Doodle your own Stirling Head and colour it in. Who will you draw?

2005: Modern craftspeople used her illustrations when making new versions, which you can now see in the Stirling Heads Gallery. Each took a month to make! Without Jane Ferrier, the missing Stirling Heads might have been lost forever.

Where's Isla?

Unicorns at Stirling

The legendary unicorn is Scotland's national animal. There are lots to spot at Stirling Castle, from the famous unicorn in the Stirling Tapestries to golden statues perching on top of the Great Hall.

1400s: Unicorns became part of Scotland's royal coat of arms. They represented power and wildness.

1540s: James V showed he was proud of unicorns – and that he was very rich – by hanging tapestries of them in the Royal Palace. Tapestries cost as much as a warship!

2000s: Since James V's original tapestries were long lost, weavers began to make new ones. The Stirling Tapestries are based on a series of tapestries from the 1500s called *The Hunt of the Unicorn*.

Today: £2 million later, the new Stirling Tapestries were finished. You can admire them in the Royal Palace, just like James V gazed at his unicorn tapestries hundreds of years ago.

Search and find

There are seven unicorn tapestries hanging in Stirling Castle.
This one is called 'The Unicorn is Found'. Can you find the details below?

 3 2 1

 1 1 3

Where's Isla?

What to Wear

In the 1500s, clothes revealed a lot about a person: what their job was, how rich they were, and if they were royal. Poor people wore rough cloth, nobles wore satin and velvet, and only royals were allowed to wear purple.

The **queen**, Marie de Guise, always dressed magnificently in silk gowns covered in jewels and embroidery.

A **lady-in-waiting** was a noble who helped the queen. She also wore beautiful clothes, but was not allowed to outshine her mistress.

Jesters dressed in brightly coloured silly costumes to make people laugh. Most **jesters** were men, but Marie de Guise's was a woman called Senat!

What am I missing?

Oh no! Everyone in the courtyard has lost something that belongs to them. Can you match the person to the object?

Royal courts all over Europe would send each other dolls dressed in the latest clothes, so nobles could see what fashionable people were wearing abroad.

Heralds were high-status servants who passed on messages, organised celebrations and announced guests. They wore smart uniforms.

Decorative artists made the palace look beautiful. Their aprons protected their clothes from paint splodges!

Rich people wore scented pomanders (balls of perfume) to keep bad smells away.

Clothes were washed in stale urine! 'Red-shanked girls' (meaning 'red-legged girls') got their name because they got cold, red legs from doing the laundry outside.

Where's Isla?

Young Mary, Queen of Scots

Mary, Queen of Scots lived at Stirling Castle from when she was a baby until she was 5, and probably spent a lot of time in the chambers of her mother, Marie de Guise.

Mary became queen at just 6 days old because her father, James V, died. It wasn't until she was 9 months old that Mary was crowned in Stirling Castle's Chapel Royal. She cried the whole time!

Because she was queen, Mary got the best food. Ordinary children mostly had water and porridge, but Mary drank milk and ate yummy pies!

Royalty didn't look after their children themselves. Mary's governess and maids took care of her.

Colouring time!

Colour in Mary's dress to make it fit for a queen.

Marie de Guise had chambers in the Royal Palace. This one is called the Queen's Bedchamber.

As well as reading and writing, young Mary practised dancing, singing and embroidery. She also learned French.

Mary might have played with toys like dolls, hobby horses and spinning tops.

KIDS WANTED FOR NASTY JOBS!

The lives of ordinary children were very different from Mary's. Most had to work, and some jobs were horrible!

5 year olds could be climbing boys or girls (chimney sweeps), who might get stuck or lost. It's said that one went up the Royal Palace chimneys and was never seen again!

Shepherd boys sometimes had to 'pop' sheep who had eaten too much clover and were gassy. Yuck!

Young cleaners known as 'gong-scourers' had to clean out squidgy piles of people's poo and smelly pools of pee. It was so disgusting that lots of them got ill or even died.

Where's Isla?

Games and Sports

Castle life wasn't all work and no play. Royals and nobles enjoyed lots of games and sports, and everyone played football!

Young Mary, Queen of Scots enjoyed many sports, like riding and falconry. When she grew up, Mary became a big fan of golf and football.

Tennis

Ball and stick

Falconry

Football

Mary's governess once refereed a royal match.

Football was banned in the 1400s because people were playing when they should have been practising archery!

Search and find
Can you spot...?

1 × [sword] ☐
4 × [ball] ☐

2 × [bird] ☐
5 × [golf club] ☐

3 × [stick] ☐
6 × [arrow] ☐

Jousting

Archery

Golf

Bowling

Walking on stilts

Fearsome football

In the past, football was much rougher. There was only one rule: no edged weapons!

Football Rule Book
No edged weapons!

The world's oldest surviving football was found hidden in the walls of the Royal Palace. It is over 500 years old, and made of leather and a pig's bladder.

Where's Isla?

the Great Kitchens

In the Great Kitchens, an army of cooks and servants prepared magnificent feasts for the royal family and their guests.

Most cooks and kitchen servants were men.

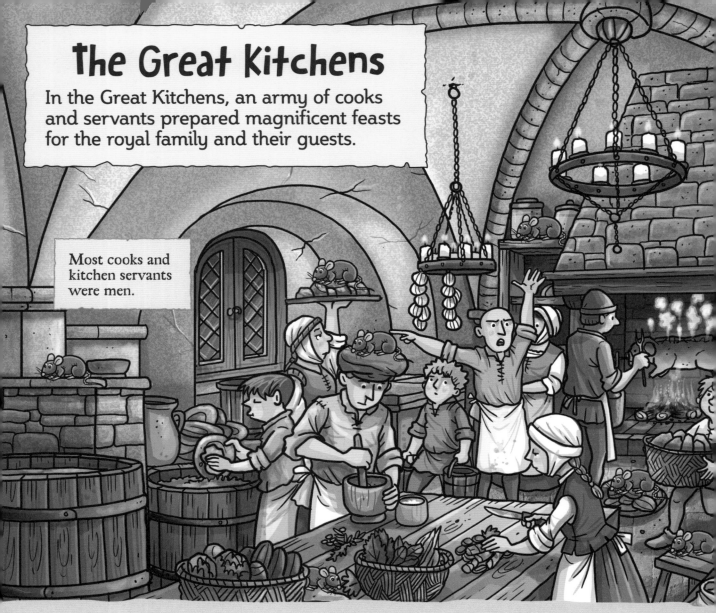

the food chain

The kitchen cooked more food than the king and queen could possibly eat. Leftovers were passed down from servant to servant until scraps reached the kitchen again. (Rats ate whatever they could find whenever they wanted!)

King and queen   Courtiers

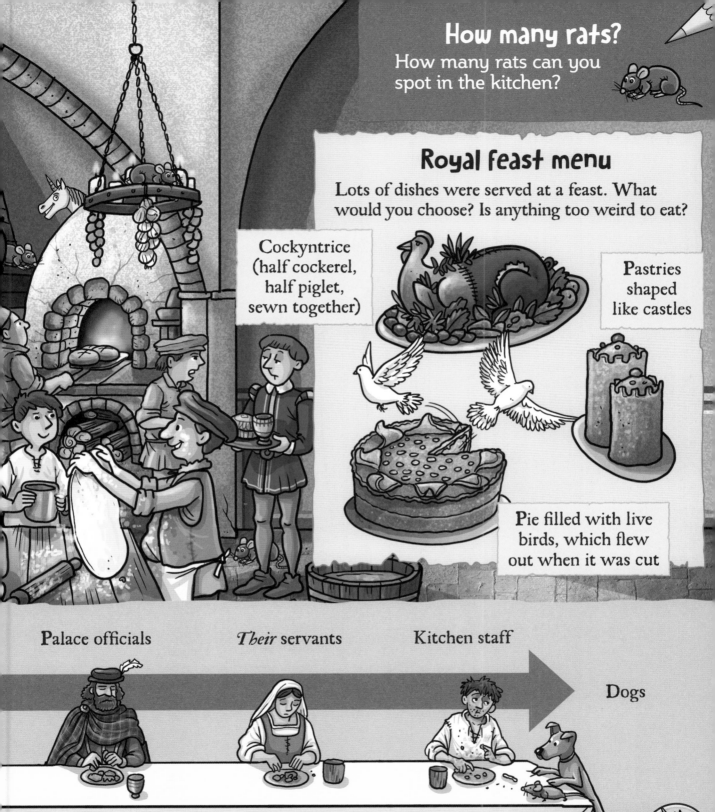

Royal feast menu

Lots of dishes were served at a feast. What would you choose? Is anything too weird to eat?

Cockyntrice (half cockerel, half piglet, sewn together)

Pastries shaped like castles

Pie filled with live birds, which flew out when it was cut

Palace officials

Their servants

Kitchen staff

Dogs

Where's Isla?

Celebrations at Stirling

Kings and queens hosted wonderful feasts and dances in the Great Hall. In 1594, James VI celebrated the baptism of his baby son, Prince Henry, with a grand banquet. Some of the food was served from a huge model ship!

The banquet was sea-themed because James VI had sailed all the way to Denmark to marry the baby prince's mother, Anna, who became queen.

Entertainers dressed up as mermaids and sea gods.

The ship was a model, but the cannons – and their noise – were real!

The Great Hall's amazing hammerbeam roof was made from 400 oak trees, 3,000 wooden pegs, and not one nail! It slotted together like a huge 3D jigsaw.

The king and queen sat on a raised platform so everyone could see them.

The fish weren't real: they were made of sugar.

James VI's own baptism was also amazing. His mother, Mary, Queen of Scots, held 3 days of celebrations for him, including a pretend siege of an enchanted castle.

James VI had the castle's old chapel knocked down and a new one built for Prince Henry's baptism. The builders had to work very quickly and it was finished in only 7 months! The Chapel Royal still stands today.

Where's Isla?

Gruesome Castle

Stirling Castle has some scary secrets. Find out about mysterious skeletons, a shocking murder, and a king who was afraid of witches!

In 1997, ten skeletons were dug up under an old chapel. This was strange because people were not usually buried in the castle. Historians and scientists think two of the skeletons were probably warriors killed in battle in the 1300s. They also discovered...

...that one big **male skeleton** was a knight. He had lots of injuries, including a scar on his head from an axe wound.

...that an archer might have killed him, because an arrowhead was found with his bones.

...what both of them looked like because scientists used computers to piece their skulls together like jigsaws!

...a **female skeleton**. She might have been a warrior!

...holes in her skull that show she may have been hit by a poleaxe or war hammer.

1452: During dinner with the Earl of Douglas, King James II lost his temper with his friend, stabbed him **29** times then threw his body out of a window!

1590s: James VI was terrified of witches. Witch marks that looked like flowers were carved into the Royal Palace doors to scare them off.

Complete the picture

You've discovered bones underneath the castle! Draw the other half of the skeleton.

Where's Isla?

Bang! Cannons and Weapons

After royalty stopped living at Stirling Castle, it became a place for soldiers to stay. By the 1800s, guns and cannons became the main weapons used in battle. To fire them you needed highly explosive gunpowder. It was kept safely in special rooms called powder magazines, because one wrong move and... BANG!

POWDER MAGAZINE RULES

Follow these rules to avoid EXPLOSIONS!

Flames = explosions.
Do not strike matches!

Boots can make sparks! Take them off and put on special slippers before coming inside.

Do not smoke pipes or cigars!

Windows must be closed during thunderstorms!

PRISON for all rule-breakers!

Find a route through the maze

Can you get out of the powder magazine maze without setting off an explosion?

Start

Finish

Crossbows vs cannons

There was a big difference between the weapons wielded by warriors defending Stirling Castle during the Wars of Independence and those carried by soldiers stationed there in the 1800s. Who do you think would win: warriors with swords and crossbows or soldiers with guns and cannons?

Crossbow

Cannon

Musket

Pike

Sword

Pistol

Where's Isla?

True or False?

Lots of unbelievable things have happened at Stirling Castle, but only one of these facts is actually false. Which one is made up?

In 1314, Robert the Bruce burned down Stirling Castle so enemy troops couldn't use it if they recaptured it!

Long ago, people thought unicorns had magical healing powers. Sometimes sailors sold pretend unicorn horns that were really narwhal tusks!

Royal kids weren't always well behaved. James VI's son Prince Henry cheekily carved graffiti about his dad into the walls!

James V used to ride around the Royal Palace on his pet lion. He enjoyed leaping out from behind walls and frightening people!

Mary, Queen of Scots had four best friends – and they were all called Mary too!

Answers

Choose the right route (p. 5)

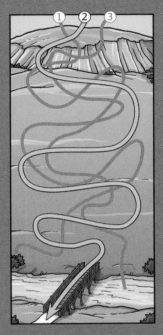

Spot the difference (p. 11)

Search the court (pp. 8–9)

Search and find (p. 15)

What am I missing? (pp. 16–17)

Search and find (pp. 20–21)

How many rats? (pp. 22–23)

How many shells? (pp. 24–25)

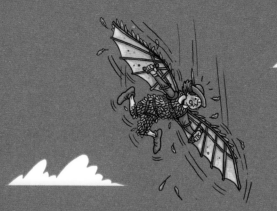

Find a route through the maze (p. 29)

True or False? (p. 30)

B is the made-up fact!

Wherever you are from, finding out about the past helps us all to understand the present. With thanks to my friends at Floris Books. – M.C.

Printed on sustainably sourced FSC® paper.

Uses plant-based inks which reduces chemical emissions and makes this book easier to recycle.

Kelpies is an imprint of Floris Books. First published by Floris Books, Edinburgh in 2022. Text © 2022 Floris Books. Illustrations © 2022 Moreno Chiacchiera. Moreno Chiacchiera asserts his right under the Copyright, Designs and Patents Act 1988 to be recognised as the Illustrator of this Work. All rights reserved. No part of this book may be reproduced without prior permission of Floris Books, Edinburgh www.florisbooks.co.uk British Library CIP Data available ISBN 978-178250-711-6. Printed in Great Britain by Bell & Bain Ltd

FSC
www.fsc.org
MIX
Paper from responsible sources
FSC® C007785